# Doctor

Published in the United States by
QEB Publishing, Inc.
3 Wrigley, Suite A
Irvine, CA 92618

www.qeb-publishing.com

Library of Congress Cataloging-in-Publication Data

Askew, Amanda.
   Doctor / by Amanda Askew ; illustrated by
Andrew Crowson.
         p. cm. --  (QEB people who help us)
   ISBN 978-1-59566-994-0 (hardcover)
  1.  Physicians--Juvenile literature.  I. Crowson,
Andrew, ill. II. Title.
   R690.A75 2010
   610--dc22

2009001989

ISBN 978-1-59566-710-6 (paperback)

Printed and bound in China

Words in bold are explained in the glossary on page 24.

**Author** Amanda Askew
**Designer and Illustrator** Andrew Crowson
**Consultants** Shirley Bickler and Tracey Dils

**Publisher** Steve Evans
**Creative Director** Zeta Davies
**Managing Editor** Amanda Askew

# Doctor

Amanda Askew
Andrew Crowson

QEB

QEB Publishing

Meet Amar. He is a doctor. He helps to make sick people feel better.

4

When Dr. Amar arrives at the office, Tanya is there. Tanya looks after the office and makes sure that everything is ready for when the **patients** arrive.

"Here's your mail."
"Thanks, Tanya."

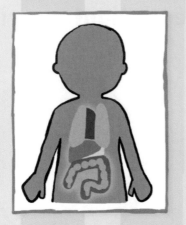

Dr. Amar goes into his office. He has a desk, chairs, cupboards, and an examination table.

He looks at his computer to check which patients he will see today.

Dr. Amar's first patient is Rosie. She has a sore throat and a **fever**.

"Your throat is very red with yellow spots. You'll have to have a few days off school and take some **medicine**."

Dr. Amar prints out a **prescription** from the computer and hands it to Rosie's dad.

"Please get this medicine from the **pharmacist**."

Next, Edward comes in. He has been getting headaches when he watches television or reads the newspaper.

Dr. Amar gives him an eye test.

"A, T... the others are a little blurry."

"I'd like you to visit an **optician** to see if you need glasses. Then come back to see me if you're still getting headaches."

AT
FYH
UPOT
OAPD
ZXJMYU
AGQBHS

11

Dr. Amar sees about 15 people in the morning, but not everyone is ill.

Last week, Jane fell off her bicycle and cut her arm deeply. She has come back to see Dr. Amar today to check that her arm is **healing** properly.

"It's looking good. I'll put a clean **bandage** on and see you again next week."

Next, Rory and his younger brother come in for a check-up.

Rory is five years old.
"Hello Rory. Step on
the scale for me.
You weigh 40 pounds.
You're growing quickly!"

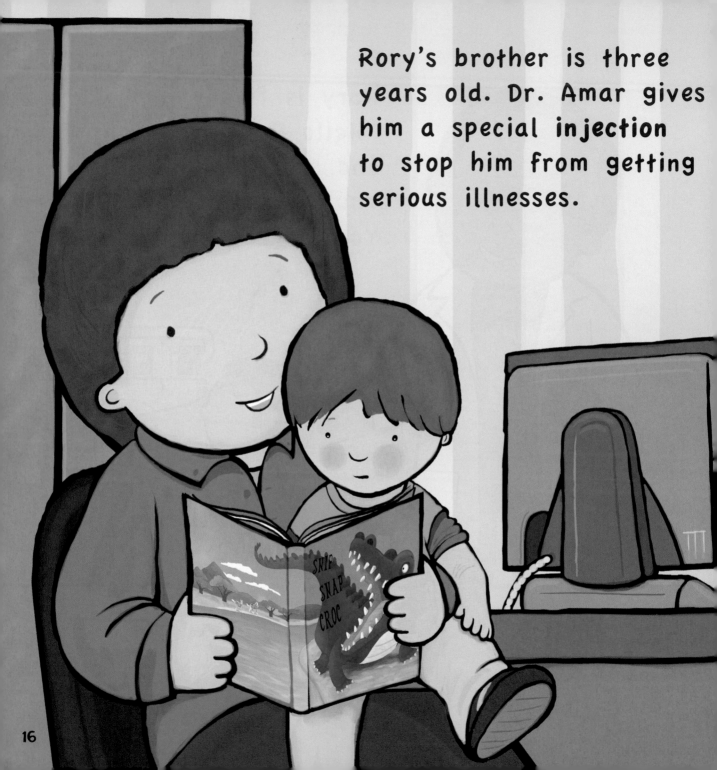

Rory's brother is three years old. Dr. Amar gives him a special **injection** to stop him from getting serious illnesses.

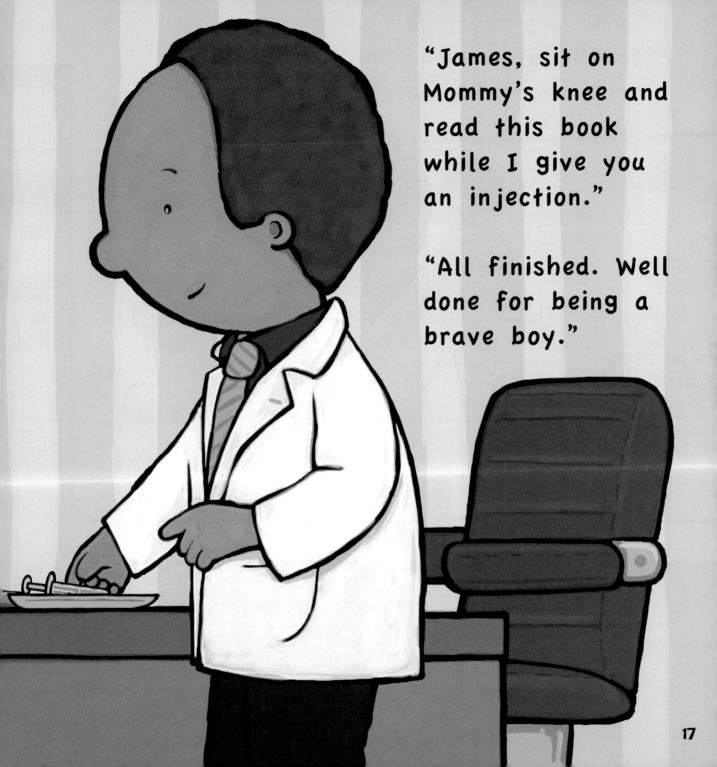

"James, sit on Mommy's knee and read this book while I give you an injection."

"All finished. Well done for being a brave boy."

In the afternoon, Dr. Amar
sees about 15 more people.

Salma has itchy **eczema** on her arms
that she cannot stop scratching.

Peter has a terrible earache.

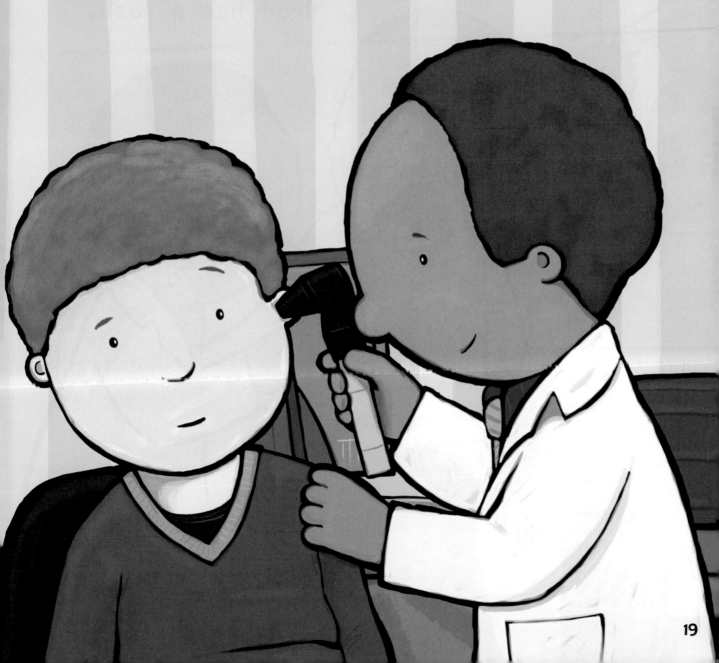

Brad has a rash.

Susi has a
tickly cough.

21

Finally, Dr. Amar sees Tom. He has banged his thumb with a hammer. It's very red and swollen.

Dr. Amar cleans his thumb and wraps it in a bandage.

"Come back to see me if the swelling does not go down in a few days."

# Glossary

**Bandage** A piece of cloth that is tied around a cut to protect it.

**Eczema** Where the skin is very red, swollen and itchy.

**Fever** A high temperature.

**Heal** When skin or bone grows back and becomes healthy again.

**Injection** Where a needle is used to put medicine into someone's body.

**Medicine** A liquid that someone drinks to get well.

**Optician** Someone who checks that people can see properly.

**Patient** Someone who visits a doctor when they are sick.

**Pharmacist** A shop that sells medicine.

**Prescription** A piece of paper that tells a pharmacist which medicine someone needs.